The Israeli and Palestinian Conflict

THE UNTOLD STORY YOU NEED TO KNOW

Michael James

TABLE OF CONTENT

CHAPTER THIRTEEN   155

CONCLUSION   161

INTRODUCTION

What is the war between Israel and Palestine about?
The endless battle between Israel and Palestine is ongoing because of the dispute on the ownership of Jerusalem.

Who owns Jerusalem?

This question begs an answer. We all want to know the answer now. Everyone is heavily interested because we want peace in the Middle East. The war in the region of the Middle East has gone on for decades. Some people have grown up with conflict from the Middle East as a

norm. It has probably gone on longer than we think.

Is peace a possibility to this war that continues to

Rage on?

What could be the reason for a persistent war/conflict

Does that seem to be going nowhere?

What is the bone of contention?

The land in question over which there have been constant conflicts between Palestine and Israel has belonged to so many nations for decades.

At some point in history, the land was owned by Persia.

Then next, it was the Turks who owned it.

Over the years, massive immigration of Jews from Poland occurred, and everyone left except the Jews. They seemed to be the only ethnic group who have stayed in Jerusalem from inception. Many believe that the solution to their problem is equity. The Jews once gave up Gaza and the Golan Height. They also offered Arafat 88% of the West Bank, all in a bid to have peace.

Palestinian leaders are insistent on owning 100%, and the Jews do not intend to give away 100%. To give away a 100% of the land is to cease to exist. It would mean the destruction of the Jews.

Will war give way for negotiation? Will negotiation give way to war?

Let us find out the history of Jerusalem.

CHAPTER ONE

Israel and Palestine

A Brief history
Israel

According to Wikipedia, the land of Israel is also known as the Holy Land of Palestine. Israel is the birthplace of the Jews. It is also the place where Judaism and Christianity were birthed.

There are sites in Israel sacred to Christianity, Islam, Judaism, Samaritanism, Druze, and Baha'i faith.

The geographical location has come under the ruler-ship

of many different empires and has been home to many other ethnic groups over the years.

The land was mainly Jewish, an outgrowth of Canaanites at approximately 1000 years before known as the Common Era.

In the 4th century, the Roman Empire adopted Christianity, resulting in a Greco-Roman Christian majority that lasted until the 7th century.

In the 7th century, Arab Muslims conquered the geographical location known as Israel. It became predominantly Muslim for the next six centuries.

In the 13th century, Arabic was the lingua franca in that

location and it continued to dominantly Muslim, ending the Crusader period (1099-1291).

The conflict was ongoing between Christians and Muslims in this era. It was part of the Syrian province under the Mamluk sultanate, and then in 1516, it became part of the Ottoman Empire until the British conquered it in 1917-1918.

Palestine

Palestine is derived from the Greek word Philistia.

It dates back to the descriptions given by ancient Greek writers in the 12th century BC.

The books record that it is a small region of land that has a prominent role in the ancient and modern history of the Middle East. It is popularly known for land disputes and political conflict throughout history. It is crucial to many essential world religions.

It represents the crossroads between Asia and Africa.

Her people consist of Arabs and are known as Palestinians. They claim that they desire to create a free and independent state in that location.

In theory, Palestine includes the West Bank and Gaza Strip, although they do not have absolute control over this area. It is complicated.

Over 135 countries recognize Palestine as an independent

have discovered Neanderthal, and early modern human remains.

A female skeleton named Tabun, viewed as one of the most important human fossils, was found here.

Their findings helped them prove that humans have existed for roughly a million years.

House of David

In the second millennium BCE, the New Kingdom of Egypt from C1550 to C1180 dominated Canaan, who became Israel later. The first recorded battle took place in 1457 BCE at Megiddo. It was a battle between the Canaanite army and the Pharaoh in Egypt,

Thutmose III. It was recorded by the scribe of the pharaoh, Tianeni. The tine of the early Israelites is known in history as the Iron Age I. The first time Israel is acknowledged in history is at Merneptah stele.

Historian William G Dever says that Israel was more of a

cultural or political entity than a state. He claims that Israel's ancestors may have included Semites native to Canaan. In the middle of the Iron Age I, a population of people, began to identify as Israel and has characteristics such as family history, genealogy, and religion. They also prohibited inter-marriage.

Writing in Hebrew

The first use of graphene-based writing began in the area around which Israel was located. It is said to be among Canaanite people who were residents in Egypt.

This form of writing changed into the Phoenician alphabet. The use of the Paleo Hebrew alphabet dates back to 1000 BCE. The language in use at the time was biblical Hebrew.

The City of David in Jerusalem

From the Bible, we see the story of Samson and David, and Goliath and have a feel of the conflict that has existed between Israel and Palestine goes back centuries.

The capital of philistines in Bible times is Gaza.

We understand that the Philistines were Greek refugee settlers who lived on the South Levantine coast from the Bible. David, King Solomon, and every other king who ruled after them are referenced in the Torah, the Bible, and the Koran.

From the Bible, it is understood that sometime around 930 BCE, Solomon had died, and the kingdom split into Judah and Israel via internal disputes.

From the book of Kings, when the split happened, the Egyptian pharaoh 'Shishaq' took advantage, invaded Israel, and plundered Jerusalem.

There is not much archaeological evidence, so many scholars suggest that this part of the Bible, written 200 years later, was exaggerated.

They imply that the writers wanted to exaggerate the importance of the House of David.

Two inscriptions, one on the Tel Dan Stele and the Mesha Stele and the other on the Moabite Stele describe the invasion of Moab by King Omri in 840 BCE.

Jehu, son of Omri, some of his wars of note, were recorded in the Assyrian records.

Numerous instances of modern archaeological findings show that Samaria was large. Some scholars have suggested that the biblical account of David and Solomon is the work of the Judean leader's effort to ascribe Israel's triumphs to the reign of King David.

New Words

Megiddo: It is known in Greek as Armageddon.

Phoenician alphabet: It is the origination of all modern alphabets.

The Moabite Stele is now in the Louvre.

The Assyrian records are now in the British Museum

Babylon Sacks Jerusalem, Makes It a Pagan City

The Bible recognizes the season that the people of Israel were carried into Babylon via Daniel and the three Hebrew boys in the book of Daniel in the Bible. One other occasion was when Esther married the king of

Babylon.

Assyrians, Persians, Greeks, Babylonians, and Romans historically occupied the geographical location known as Palestine. Some other nations that fought and won a ruler-ship over Palestine were Arabs, Fatimids, Crusaders, Turks, Seljuk, Egyptians, and Mamelukes.

The Ottoman Empire ruled most of Palestine from the time duration of 1517 to 1917.

The Kingdoms of Israel and Judah

In 854 BCE, an alliance was made between Ahab of Israel and Ben Hadad II of Aram Damascus, and they went to battle and rebuffed the invasions of the Assyrians. It is the battle of Qargar. The Assyrian records (also called the Kukah Monoliths) back these facts.

Historians say that these events were not included in the Bible.

Tiglath-Pileser III, an Assyrian king in 750BCE, destroyed the kingdom of Israel. The Assyrians also destroyed the Philistine kingdom.

Assyrians then sent most of the surviving population of Israel into exile. This created the story of the "Lost Tribes of Israel."

Samaritans claim to be originated from the survivors of the Assyrian conquest. Around 724-722BCE, all the Israelite revolts were destroyed after King Sargon of Assyria captured Samaria.

Scholars say that surviving Jews moved to Judah, causing Jerusalem to expand and lead to the construction of the Siloam Tunnel. This was done during the rule of King Hezekiah at 715-686BCE. This was the source of water for the Jews during the siege. The Bible backs this fact.

Archaeological teams also discovered a Hebrew plaque that the team of constructor workers left there.

King Sennacherib is the son of King Sargon. He did not succeed in conquering Judah when Hezekiah was reigning.

According to Assyrian records, Sennacherib leveled 46 walled cities and held Jerusalem in a siege and only left after he got an all-encompassing tribute.

The Bible backs the facts about the tribute, saying that

Hezekiah allied with Tahoraa, the King of Kush. The Twenty-Fifth Dynasty of

Egypt most likely defeated the Assyrians. To celebrate his victory at Lachish, Sennacherib had a 12 by 5-meter frieze erected in his palace at Nineveh. The Bible describes a culture of prophets who speak for God and give rulers the counsel of God. The most famous of them was Isaiah, and he witnessed the Assyrian invasion and warned Israel of what God would do.

NEW WORDS

The Twenty-Fifth Dynasty of Egypt was also known as the Nubian Pharaohs.

Kush – Modern-day Sudan

Nineveh is modern-day Iraq.

Lachish is the second-largest city in Judah.

Jews Exiled to Babylon

The Route of the Exiles to Babylon

Nebuchadnezzar II of Babylon conquered Judah in 586BCE.

From the Bible, there are details on how he destroyed the Temple Solomon built and exiled the Jews to Babylon.

The Philistines also went to Babylon in exile. According to Babylonian chronicles, it is suggested that the King of Judah, Jehoiachin, broke his agreement with Babylon and made a new one with Egypt.

Babylon punished him by invading Judah.

Amidst the ruins of Babylon, archaeologists discovered tablets that described the rations assigned to the king. From the Bible and the Talmud, records are showing that the lineage of David continued to the head of the Jews amongst those exiled in Babylon.

They were called the "Rosh Galut."

The classification of Rosh Galut continued for 1500 and stopped in the 11th century.

Obverse of Yehud Silver Coin

Cyrus the Great of Persia conquered Babylon and inherited everything that belonged to him. After a time, Cyrus issued a decree that granted the nations that paid tribute to his freedom.

From the Bible, we learn that more than 50,000 Jews returned to Judah under the leadership of Zerubbabel. On their return, they rebuilt the temple that the Babylonians destroyed.

Around the same time, another 5000 Jews, led by Ezra and Nehemiah, returned to Judah in 456 BCE. Non-Jews had written to Cyrus to try to prevent their return, but they were unsuccessful.

Modern scholars are of the school of thought that the final Hebrew versions of the Torah and Books of Kings have similar dates when the Israelites returned. The Jews then adopted the Aramaic script from Babylon, which is the current Hebrew script. The Babylonian calendar and the Hebrew calendar are similar.

The Persians conquered Egypt and posted a Judean military garrison on Elephantine Island near Aswan.

One hundred seventy-five papyrus documents were discovered in the 20th Century. It recorded activities of the community, including details on how to carry out Passover, a very important culture of the Jews.

Alexander, the Great of Macedonia, defeated Persia and conquered their entire region in 333 BCE. In his death, his generals fought over the conquered territory, and Judah was made the frontier between Egypt and the Seleucid Territory. It eventually became a part of the Seleucid territory in 200 BCE.

This was the battle of Panium.

In the 3rd Century, the first translation of the Hebrew Bible, the Greek Septuagint, was made. This was during the rule of Ptolemy II Philadelphus. It was made for the library of Alexandria.

Hasmonean Kingdom

The Seleucid ruler Antiochus IV Epiphanes attempted to eradicate Judaism in favor of Hellenistic religion. This was in the 2nd Century BCE.

A Maccabean Revolt occurred Judas Maccabeus led that. The books of the Maccabees describe the revolt and mark the end of Greek rule.

Meanwhile, a Jewish sect called the Hasideans supported neither the revolt nor Hellenism and reluctantly backed the Maccabees.

The Hasmonean dynasty of Jewish priest-kings was responsible for ruling Judah and eth Essenes, Pharisees, and Sadducees. They were the foremost Jewish social movements.

Simon ben Shetach was a Pharisee leader who built the first set of schools around meeting houses. They were built for opposing Hellenistic civilization.

The Sanhedrin administered justice. The leader of the Sanhedrin was Nasi. His religious authority eventually superseded that of the Temple high priest, a king under the Hasmonean rule.

The Hasmonean influence grew until they had control over the region. By 125 BCE, the Hasmonean ethnarch John Hyrcanus brought Edom under the rule of the Hasmonean and converted its populations to Judaism.

The son of Hyrcanus son Alexander Jannaeus developed good relations with the Roman Republic.

Unfortunately, the Pharisees and Sadducees were unhappy and conflicted over the succession to Jannaeus. They thus invited foreign intervention.

NEW WORDS

Aramaic script is also known as the Ashuri alphabet.

The battle of Panium was fought near Banias on the Golan Heights).

The victory in the Maccabean Revolt is celebrated in the Jewish culture of Hanukkah.

CHAPTER THREE

The Jews in Rome

Pompey, the Roman General, conquered Syria in 64BCE. He also intervened in the civil war brewing in Jerusalem and restored Hyrcanus II as High Priest, making Judah a vassal of Rome.

Three thousand Hyrcanus sent 3000 troops to save Julius Caesar and Cleopatra during the siege of Alexander in 47BCE. The commander of the troops we Antipater and Caesar, made his descendants King of Judah as a reward.

PORTION OF THE TEMPLE SCROLL, ONE OF THE DEAD SEA SCROLLS WRITTEN BY THE ESSENES

Descendants of Antipater were the Jewish Roman client kings who ruled from 37 to 6 BCE. Herod the Great enlarged his temple, and it was one of the most revered religious structures of the world at the time.

The Jews were as much as 10 percent of the Roman empire at this time. They also had large communities of Jews in North Africa and Arabia.

Rabbinical Judaism with Hillel in leadership became popular despite the fame of the temple Herod built.

The Jewish temple in Jerusalem had the permission not to display an effigy of the Emperor. Judaism was the only religious structure in the Roman Empire that received an exemption.

The Jewish citizens had a special consideration from the Roman Empire to pay a tax to the temple.

Augustus made Judea a Roman Province in 6CE. He deposed Herod Archelaus and appointed a Roman governor.

Judas of Galilee led a revolt against Roman taxation, and in the decades following the Greco-Romans, and Judah's populations, there was conflict. There was resistance to putting an effigy of Emperor Caligula in Synagogues and the Jewish temple.

In the last year of Herod's rule, Jesus was born in the Judean city of Bethlehem, as corroborated by the Bible.

Pontius Pilate executed Jesus in Jerusalem between 25 and 35CE. All his followers, the apostles, and Paul all through 5-67CE were busy speaking about the kingdom of God and acknowledging Jesus as the "Son of God."

In 50CE, Jerusalem abandoned the Jewish requirement of circumcision and created a different form of Judaism that was more acceptable to non-Jews. It is believed that Peter became the first pope.

Christians Sack Jerusalem, they Kill the Jews & Muslims

Siege of Jerusalem

The Jews who lived in Judea revolted against Rome in 66CE and named their new state Israel.

Historian and Jewish leader Josephus narrated the events as they happened. He detailed the defense at Jotapata, the siege at Jerusalem, and the desperate last stand at Masada. All of this happened under the leadership of Eleazar ben Yair between 72- 73 CE.

Most of Jerusalem and the temple were destroyed.

At the time of the Jewish revolt, most of the Christians removed themselves from Judea.

The Pharisee's association under Yochanan ben Zakai made peace with Rome and survived. The war ended, and the Jews continued to pay tribute to the Fiscus Judaicus. This was used to find a temple to Jupiter. The Romans, in memory of their victory, erected an arch. It still stands today.

There were more attacks, and these led to a massive uprising against Rome from 115-117CE. All the Jews in Cyprus, Libya, Egypt, and Mesopotamia fought in this battle. There were massacres on both sides.

The Jewish population in Cyprus all disappeared, and new settlers were brought in, and Jews were disqualified from living in Cyprus.

Jerusalem was renamed "*Aelia Capitolina*" by Emperor Hadrian in 131 CE.

A temple dedicated to Jupiter was constructed on the site of the Jewish temple. Jews were disqualified from living in Jerusalem. The disqualification lasted until the Arab conquest.

The Roman province known as Judaea Province was renamed Palaestina.

Five years later, Simon Bar Kokhba, another Jewish leader, led another foremost revolt against the Romans. The country was again renamed Israel. This revolt caused more trouble for the Romans. Christians did not participate in the revolt, and the Jews began to see Christianity as a different religion.

Emperor Hadrian shattered the revolt. During the revolt, a rabbinical assembly decided to exclude the Apocrypha and Christian books from the Hebrew bible. This explains why some Hebrew texts and the Books of Maccabees are lost.

After the 136 CE Jewish Defeat

The Romans shattered the Bar Kochba revolt and exiled the Jews from Judah. They allowed a rabbinical patriarch called Nasi to represent the Jews in their meetings. The most famous of their leaders is Judah haNasi, and he is credited with compiling the Mishnah and demanding that illiterates Jews be treated as outcasts.

There was rivalry between Palestinian and Babylonian academies. Palestine belonged to the school of thought that leaving the land in a time of peace was idolatry. Babylonian scholars belonged to the school of thought that the rabbis from Palestine were inferior.

The heavy taxation and crisis in the economy that rocked those times were used in financing wars, affecting the 3rd Century Roman Empire. This resulted in more Jews emigrating from Syria Palaestina to Persia Sassanid Empire, a territory that was more favorable as Jews prospered there. They had many seminaries in Babylon.

NEW WORD

The names "Palestine" (in English) and "Filistin" (in Arabic) were derived from the new name Palaestina.

CHAPTER FOUR

Rome Adopts Christianity

In the 4th Century, Emperor Constantine made Constantinople the capital of the East Roman Empire. Christianity became acceptable. His mother, Helena, traveled on the holy pilgrimage to Rome in 326-328CE.

She led the construction of the nativity, the grave and built other key churches.

The name of Jerusalem has changed once again to Aelia Capitolina. It became a Christian city. Jews were not permitted to live in Jerusalem. They were permitted to visit and worship at the site of the destroyed temple.

The Christians spent the next 100 years committed to eradicating paganism, and this led to the demolition of Roman traditions and the destruction of its temples. At the end of the 4th Century, if you were caught worshipping pagan gods, you executed, and your property impounded.

Another Jewish revolt in Galilee broke out against a corrupt Roman governor in 351-352 CE.

A pagan Roman Emperor, Julian the Apostate, announced plans to rebuild the Jewish temple in 363 CE. The project was discontinued when he died fighting the Persians in the same year.

Emperor Theodosius I, the last Emperor of the Roman Empire, made Christianity the official religion. This happened in 380CE.

The Roman Empire split in 390CE, and the territory became a part of the Christian East Roman Empire. It was called the Byzantine Empire.

The Greek Eastern Orthodox Church dominated Byzantine Christianity. Its land ownership extends to the present.

The Western Roman Empire collapsed in the Fifth Century, leading to the migration of the Christians to the Roman province of Palaestina Prima. A Christian majority developed.

The Jews were as much as 10-15% of the population and lived mostly around Galilee.

The only non-Christian religion tolerated was Judaism. Slowly the restrictions inflicted on the Jews increased to an embargo on building new places of worship, owning Christian slaves, or holding a public office.

Following the death of the last Nasi, Gamliel VI, the title of Nasi was banned, and the Sanhedrin was abolished.

More revolts mark the period, resulting in the reduction in the Samaritan population from a million to almost extinct.

The Gemara, the Jerusalem Talmud, and the Passover Haggadah are sacred Jewish texts written in this period.

Mar-Zutra II set up an independent Jewish state in 495CE. Today, it is modern-day Iraq. It lasted seven years till it fell. After its fall, his son, Mar-Zutra III, moved to Tiberias and became head of the local religious academy in 520 CE.

The Romans took the Jewish Menorah when the temple was destroyed. Vandals took it to Carthage after Rome was sacked in 455 CE.

Byzantine historian, Procopius, says that the Byzantine army recovered the Jewish Menorah and brought it to Constantinople.

Khosrow II, the ruler of Sassanid Persia, invaded the Byzantine Empire in 611 BCE. He allied with Jewish fighters who Benjamin of Tiberias conscripted. They captured Jerusalem in 614 CE.

The Persians captured the "True Cross." The Jewish Himyarite Kingdom in Yemen was also an ally of the ruler of Sassanid Persia.

Nehemiah ben Hushiel became the governor of Jerusalem.

Christian historians claim the Jews massacred the Christians in the city. There is no archaeological evidence of such an event.

Kavad II, the son of Khosrow, returned Palestine and the True Cross to Byzantines, signing a peace pact with them in 628.

With the return of Byzantine, Heraclius massacred the Jewish population in Galilee, and Jews were once again banned from entering Jerusalem.

Benjamin of Tiberias converted to Christianity.

NEW WORDS

Helena built a church of the nativity in Bethlehem and a church of the Holy Sepulchre, where Jesus was buried in Jerusalem amongst other churches.

Saladin, a Muslim, Sacks Christians From Jerusalem

EARLY MUSLIM PERIOD

Muslim tradition holds that on the night that Mohammed died, he was taken from Mecca to the farthest mosque. Many believe it was the Temple Mount. They also believe that he returned on the same night.

Muawiyah led an Arab army and conquered Palestine plus the entire Levant in 635. He made it a province of the new Medina-based Arab Empire.

The ban the Byzantine placed on the Jews ended. Muslims began to dominate Palestine, despite Christianity being the dominant religion because of the Crusaders.

Muawiyah has crowned the Caliph in Jerusalem, making him the first of the Umayyad dynasty in 661.

Umayyad Abd al-Malik constructed what is known as the Dome of the Rock shrine on the Temple Mount in 691.

The Temple Mount is the place where the Jewish temple once stood. He also erected the Al-Aqsa Mosque at the same spot in 705.

These same buildings were built again in the 10th Century after being destroyed by a series of earthquakes.

To the Muslims, the Temple Mount is a place that contains the Foundation Stone.

The Jews believe that it is the site where Abraham sacrificed his son, Isaac, to the Lord. This is in the place called Mecca.

Ramlah was built in the Muslim Capital, Jund Filastin. In 750, there arose discrimination against non-Arabs. This led to Abbasid Revolution, and a people called Abbasid Caliphs replaced the Umayyads. They built Baghdad, and it became their capital.

Caliph Umar II introduced a new law in the 8th Century. This required that Jews and Christians wear clothing that identified them as such. The Jews were required to wear yellow stars as a necklace and on their hats. The Christians were required to wear blue. This was not enforced all the time. It was enforced only during periods when they wanted to humiliate or persecute non-Arabs.

All non-Muslims had to pay taxes as ordered by Islamic rulers. The punishment for non-payment was imprisonment. They were disqualified from traveling without presenting their tax receipt. They were disqualified from building new places of worship or renovate their existing worship places. Other areas of Europe that were Christian eventually adopted the world system requirement that Jews wear yellow stars.

Caliph Al-Aziz Billah, a member of the Cairo-based Fatimid dynasty, conquered the Muslim region in 982.

In 982, Caliph Al-Aziz Billah of the Cairo-based Fatimid dynasty conquered the region.

The Fatimids followed Isma'ilism. It is a branch of Shia Islam, and they claimed to be descendants of Mohammed, the Holy Prophet's daughter. In 1,010, the church of Holy Sepulchre (where Jesus was buried) was destroyed by Fatimid Caliph al-Hakim. Ten years later, he paid to have the Holy Sepulchre to be rebuilt. In 1020, he claimed that he was divine and was revered as a Messiah by the Druze religion.

Jewish scribes called the Masoretes who lived in Galilee and Jerusalem created the Masoretic Text, the final text of the Hebrew Bible.

NEW WORDS

The Holy Sepulchre is the burial place of Jesus Christ.

Jerusalem Becomes a Muslim City

Painting of the Siege of Jerusalem During the First Crusade

The First Crusade happened in Jerusalem in 1099.

It took the city of Jerusalem and established it as a Catholic kingdom. They called it the Kingdom of Jerusalem.

Muslims and Jews were massacred arbitrarily and or sold into slavery.

The Crusaders were in search of Jews and Muslims to eradicate them. Across Europe, the Crusaders gave the Jews the choice of conversion or death. Most Jews chose death.

The bloodshed continued until the Crusaders reached the Holy Land. A certain type of Jews called the

Ashkenazi Orthodox Jews to have a prayer to keep the death and destruction as a memorial.

Raynald of Châtillon, the recognized ruler in Transjordan, created increasing conflict with Ayyubid Sultan Saladin in 1180. This led to the crusaders being defeated in 1187 in the Battle of Hattin.

Saladin took Jerusalem peacefully and conquered most of Jerusalem. His physician, Maimonides, was a refugee from Muslim persecution in Cordoba, Spain. In Spain, all non-Muslim religions were prohibited. This marked the end of the Golden age of Jewish culture in Spain.

Maimonides possessed extensive knowledge of medical practices from Greeks and Arabs.

He wrote extensively on religion in Hebrew and Judeo-Arabic, and orthodox Jews still study his writings today. He was buried in Tiberias.

Response to the Loss of Jerusalem

The Christian world responded to the loss of Jerusalem in the form of the third crusade in 1190.

Richard the Lionheart and Saladin signed the Treaty at Jaffa in 1192. Christians were allowed to pass freely on pilgrimage to the holy sites. Meanwhile, Jerusalem remained under Muslim rule.

Jerusalem was set free from Muslim control back to Christian control when Ayyubid sultan el Kamil and the Holy Roman Emperor Frederick II signed another treaty. This resulted at the end of the Sixth Crusade.

Khwarezmian Tatars slaughtered all the Christian population in the city of Jerusalem in 1244. He drove out the Jews and burned the city down.

In 1247, the Ayyubids drove out the Khwarezmians.

The Mongols wrecked Baghdad and killed hundreds of thousands. Thirty years on, the area was the borderline of Mongol Invades and Mamluks of Egypt.

Egypt became impoverished, and its population became diminished. The Sultan Qutuz of Egypt defeated the Mongols during the battle of Ain Jalut. His successes eradicated the Crusaders finally.

The Kingdom of Acre, the last Crusader state, fell in 1291 and marked the end of the Crusades.

The Bahri Mamluk Dynasty

Mamluks ruled over Palestine until 1516, and it was a part of Syria. In Hebron, traditionally known as the home of David from the Bible, Baibars prohibited the Jews from worshipping at the Cave of the Patriarchs.

The injunctions against them remained in place until Israel conquered Palestine 700 years later.

Sultan Al-Ashraf Khalil defeated the last outposts of the Crusader rule in 1291.

The Mamluks, in line with the dogma of the Ayyubids, made the tactical choice to decimate the coastal area and make Tyre and Gaza uninhabitable. They destroyed the ports and polluted the seas.

The truth was that they feared the return of the Crusaders and wanted to prefer attacks from the sea. The areas they damaged did not recover for many years. The cities affected focused on local activities as sea activities were grounded.

CHAPTER FIVE

Persecution in Europe

With the Crusaders gone, the Jews received more persecution in Europe. When the year 1290 began, Jews began to be expelled from England. France followed closely behind England.

In the 14th Century, the Jews were blamed for the Black Death, a plague that troubled Europe. Communities of Jews in Germany, Holland, Belgium, and Switzerland were exterminated.

The largest slaughter happened in Spain. Tens of thousands of Jews were killed, and half of the Jews in Spain were forced to convert to Catholicism. The only significant European Jewish community in the 14th Century lived in Spain, Italy & Eastern Europe.

The last Muslim state was defeated in Spain in January 1942. About half a year later, the Jews in Spain were then required to convert or forfeit property.

Over one hundred thousand Jews converted, although they continued to practice Judaism covertly.

This led to the creation of the Catholic Church's inquisition. Torquemada led it. It is popularly known as the Spanish Inquisition. Any Jew found to be practicing Judaism would face a death sentence via public burning, a sentence reserved for witches.

175,000 Jews left Spain.

Columbus sailed to America on the last day the Jews were allowed to remain in Spain according to its laws.

The Jews paid a large payment, and so 100,000 Jews were allowed into Portugal. But five years later, their children were seized, and they were given the choice of converting to Christianity or leaving Portugal forcefully without their children.

Again, most of the Jews converted but practiced Judaism covertly.

The Jewish converts in Spain and Portugal experienced great economic success. The nations were suspicious of their conversion's genuineness, so this led to the creation of laws that restricted the rights of Christians of Jewish origin.

Those who helped them escape maltreated the Jews who escaped. They were refused entry at almost every port around the Mediterranean. They feared being overrun by Jews.

More expulsions happened in Italy, affecting the survivors of the first expulsion.

Many of the secret Jews decided to move to the New World. There, they were allowed to practice Judaism freely for a short time. Other Spanish Jews emigrated to Poland, North Africa, and the Ottoman Empire.

Many moved, especially to Thessaloniki. This became the world's largest Jewish city.

Some headed for Israel. At that moment in history, the Ottomans controlled Israel.

Jews living in Venice, Italy, were required to live in the Ghetto. This practice spread to the Papal States and all across Europe.

The Jews who did not live in the Ghetto had to wear a yellow star. Jews who practiced Judaism covertly were not allowed to convert back to Judaism as it carried a death sentence.

The Vatican in Rome administered the last compulsory Ghetto. This practice was abolished in the 1880s.

David Reubeni attempted to convince Emperor Charles V in 1523 to plan to begin to train a Jewish army to conquer Judea. The plan was to get the Jewish kingdom back. They planned to use Jewish warriors in India and

Ethiopia. He succeeded in meeting with a number of the royal leaders.

The inquisition executed him.

Ottoman Period

Bilad a-Sham, modern-day Syria, was conquered by the Turkish Sultan Selim in 1516-1517.

It thus became a part of the province of Ottoman Syria for four centuries. It was first the Damascus Eyalet, and then it was known as Syria Vilayet.

The Ottoman Sultans encouraged the Jewish refugees of the inquisition in Catholic Europe to settle in the Ottoman Empire.

The personal physician of Suleiman the Magnificent was called Moses Hamon. He was a survivor of the inquisition.

Many Jewish businesswomen dominated communication between the outside world and the harem.

Suleiman the magnificent ruled between 1520 and 1566. In 1535, he built the current city walls of Jerusalem. It took him six years to finish it. Jerusalem had been without walls for almost two centuries.

The successor to Suleiman was Selim II. He married a Jewish woman, Nurbanu Sultan. She gave the control of Tiberias to Dona Gracia Mendes Nasi. Dona was one of the richest women in Europe and had escaped the inquisition.

She made the Jewish refugees know that they were safe and started a Hebrew printing press.

Safed was made a center for the study of the Kabbalah. Joseph Nasi, the nephew of Dona, was made the governor of Tiberias, and he motivated Jews in Italy to travel to settle in Tiberias.

According to Jewish tradition, the Four Holy Cities are Jerusalem, Hebron, Tiberias, and Safed. During the Khmelnytsky Uprising in Ukraine, more than tens of thousands of Jews were killed.

Safed and Tiberias were destroyed in 1660 during a Druze revolt. Sabbatai Zevi settled in 1663. Nathan of Gaza declared him a Jewish Messiah. He had a large number of followers. Istanbul, Sultan Suleiman II forced him to convert to Islam.

His followers converted to Islam, and the sect exists in Turkey today. It is known as Dönmeh.

Towards the end of the 18th Century, a local Arab sheik Zahir al-Umar created a de facto independent Emirate in Galilee. Ottoman tried to conquer the Sheikh but failed. After Zahir's death, the Ottomans continued to rule over his territory.

Napoleon occupied the country for a short while in 1799. He planned a proclamation to invite the Jews to create a state.

This proclamation was abandoned when he was defeated at Acre.

Muhammad Ali of Egypt, an Ottoman ruler, left the Empire and tried to make Egypt modern in 1831. He conquered Ottoman Syria and wanted to revive and settle the regions. His policies on enlistment caused an Arab revolt in 1834. This left many casualties for the local Arab peasants. There were many massacres of Christians and Jewish communities by rebels.

After the revolt, Muhammed Ali, Muhammed Pasha, expelled about 10,000 local peasants to Egypt. He brought his loyal Egyptian soldiers and dispersed soldiers to settle the coastline of Ottoman Syria. He sent his Sudanese troops to settle Northern Jordan Valley.

Jewish Workers in Kerem Avraham Neighbourhood of Jerusalem

Another revolt by the Druze happened in 1838. Moses Montefiore met with Mohammed Pasha in Egypt. They signed an agreement to establish 100-200 Jewish villages in Damascus Eyalet of the Ottoman Empire.

In 1840, the Egyptians stepped back from the deal before implementation and gave the area governed under Ottoman.

The Jews were the largest population group in 1844.

Jews were the majority in Jerusalem in 1896. The overall population was 88% Muslim and 9% Christian

NEW WORDS

Thessaloniki is now Greece.

CHAPTER SIX

The British Sack Turks and Make Jerusalem A Royal City

The Jews in Western Europe were constantly granted citizenship and equality before the laws applicable in Western Europe.

In Eastern Europe, they faced persecution and had restrictions that were legally enforced. They were widespread pogroms, and many got raped, murdered, and lost property.

More than 50% of the world's Jews lived in the Russian Empire and were restricted to living in the Pale of Settlement.

The Empire consisted of the Poles, Lithuanians, and Ukrainians. These nations began to agitate for independence, treated the Jews as aliens and unwanted.

They spoke Yiddish.

A Jewish movement emerged within the Russian Empire. Millions of Jews fled the Empire and immigrated to the United States.

A French Jewish association created an agricultural school near Jaffa called the Alliance Israelite Universelle in 1870.

BY 1878, Jewish Emigrants in Russia established the village Petah Tikva. Another called Rishon LeZion followed this in 1882. They also established the Billy and Hovevei Zion movements. These were created to help Jewish settlers live in the community. Financial freedom was one of their goals.

They were totally unlike the Ashkenazi Jewish communities, who were very poor and depended on charity donations from other nations to live.

The French Baron, Edmond James de Rothschild, funded these new communities. His goal was to build many economic initiatives.

A vibrant community existed in Jaffa. They were wealthy, and all nationalities intermingled. More settlements and larger communities kept cropping up despite some difficulty.

The migration caused a revival of the Hebrew language, and they kept attracts Jews in their numbers. They attracted the religious, the secular, the nationalist, and the left-wing.

The Jews began to think of how to return home to Palestine as the pogroms increased in the parts of Ukraine in the Russian Empire.

When more pogroms happened in 1881, and the restrictions increased their difficulty in living, 1.9 million Russian Jews emigrated at a go. 1.5 million went to

America, the remaining went to Palestine, thus creating new communities of Jewish existence.

Between 1882 and 1903, 35,000 Jews moved to Palestine.

When the Ottoman Empire conquered their regions in 1881, Yemenite Jews were assisted by the new transportation facilities and access to other parts of the world.

In 1890, Jews were the majority in Jerusalem, although entire Palestine was mainly Muslims and Arabs of Christian faith.

Theodor Herzl published a book titled The Jewish State in Hebrew in 1896. In this book, he said that the answer to anti-Semitism in Europe was to create a Jewish state.

The Zionist Organization was founded in 1897, and at the first Zion congress, they declared that their major goal was to establish a home for the Jews in Palestine and be protected by law.

However, the Ottoman rulers were suspicious of the Jews, and so not much progress was made.

Between the years 1904 till 1914, 40,000 Jews settled in the area now known as Israel. The Zion organization set up an office known as the Palestine Bureau. It was called the Eretz Israel Office and was situated in Jaffa.

They created a systematic Jewish settlement policy.

Most of the migrants were Jews escaping persecution from Russia and Poland.

Nine Russian socialists founded the first Kibbutz, Degania, in 1909.

During the same period, residents created the first city that was Hebrew speaking. It was called Ahuzat Bayit and finally renamed Tel Aviv.

In this city, they had Hebrew schools, formed Jewish political parties, formed organizations to protect workers, and wrote Hebrew books and newspapers.

NEW WORDS

Anti-Semitism means the hatred of Jews

The British & French Divide Jerusalem, the US Approves
WORLD WAR I

World War I happened and most Jews allied with Germany. They did this because they were against the Russians who saw Jews as their enemy, many pogroms happened in Russia, and the nation treated them unjustly.

Britain sought to be allied with Jews. One reason was the influence they felt the Jews wielded in the Ottoman Empire Young Turks movement.

In Thessaloniki, 40% of the city was made of Jews. They also sought the support of Jews in America to influence the US to intervene in case Britain needed help.

British government sympathized with the goals of Zionism, including Lloyd George, the Prime minister.

More than 14,000 Jews got expelled because of the suspicion of the Ottoman military commander of the Jaffa territory in 1914-1915. He thought they were Russian sympathizers. He assumed they were hidden enemies or Zionists who wanted to detach Palestine from the Ottoman Empire.

Eventually, he expelled everyone, including the Muslims, from Jaffa and Tel Aviv in 1917. The Jews who were affected were unable to return until the British had conquered the Ottoman Empire.

When the British had succeeded in driving out the Turks from Southern Syria, Arthur Balfour, the British foreign minister, sent a public letter to British Lord Rothschild.

He was a leader of the Jewish community and a leading member of his party. This is popularly known in that era as the Balfour Declaration of 1917.

In the letter, the British declared that they favored making a home for the Jews in Palestine. This gave the British a cause for claiming and governing Palestine.

New boundaries were determined for the Middle East. There was an agreement between French and British Bureaucrats.

The Jews formed a band of men, who were mainly Zionists, and Ze'ev Jabotinsky and Joseph Trumpeldor led them. They were part of the failed Gallipoli Campaign.

The Nili Zionist spy network supplied the British with *Intel* of the Ottoman plans and the places where their troops were situated.

Interregnum

Palestine came under martial law after subduing the Ottoman Empire.

The area began to be governed by the British, French, and Arab Occupied Enemy Territory Administration. There was a truce with the Ottomans until the decree of the mandate in 1920.

The British ruler-ship of Palestine began in 1920. It was confirmed in 1922 and came into effect in 1923. Transjordan was also covered in the mandate.

Britain signed a treaty with the United States, and the terms of the mandate were endorsed by the United States.

Almost a hundred thousand Jews had been maimed or murdered in the almost 1200 pogroms in Ukraine. More Jews immigrated to Palestine between 1919 and 1923.

The Jews were trained in agriculture and created self-sustaining communities called Kibbutzim.

A Zion charity called the Jewish National Fund invested in land with money sourced from other nations.

A Jewish militia existing underground called Haganah was created. Their goal was to defend distant Jewish settlements.

Arthur Balfour visited Jerusalem to open The Hebrew University of Jerusalem on the 1st of April in 1925.

The French defeated the Arab Kingdom of Syria. The Balfour declaration led to riots in Nebi Musa and Jaffa.

To appease the Arabs, the British enforced immigration quotas on the Jews. The only Jews this was not applicable to were the wealthy Jews in possession of 1000 pounds in cash and a lot of money. Or Jewish professionals who had more than 500 pounds.

The Jewish Agency gave the British permission to come into Palestine and distributed the funds donated from wealthier Jews living in other nations.

More than 80,000 Jews running from maltreatment in Poland and Hungary immigrated to Palestine. Some forms of maltreatment were heavy taxation and some

United States laws limiting immigration from Eastern and Southern Europe.

Many of the new immigrants were middle class. They moved in and started small businesses.

Pinhas Rutenberg, a former Commissar in Russia's pre-Bolshevik Kerensky Government, built the first electric generator in 1923.

The Jewish Agency built a technological university in Haifa in 1925. The British introduced the Palestinian pound in 1927, doing away with the Egyptian pound as a currency unit.

The democratically elected Va'ad Leumi became the main institution of the Palestinian Jewish community.

As their communities grew, the Jewish National Council adopted government functions of creating health, education, healthcare, and security.

Va'ad Leumi raised his taxes and ran independent services for the Jewish population with the approval of the British. By the year 1929, Jews elected the Jewish leadership from 26 countries.

The Wailing Wall is physically located at Kotel. It is one of the holiest spots in the world for Judaism. It is a narrow alleyway, and Jews are banned from using chairs or curtains. In 1929, tensions grew over this place. The worshippers were elderly and needed seats; they also wanted to separate the men from the women.

The Mufti claimed that space as belonging to Islam, so they intentionally drove cattle through that space. They implied that the Jews were attempting to lay claim to the Temple Mount.

This caused many riots in Palestine in August 1929. Many people who were hurt were from the non-Zionist Jewish community in Hebron. They massacred them.

This caused the right-wing Zionists to create their militia in 1931.

Zionist political parties made provisions for healthcare and education. The three sects of Zionists provided healthcare and education s and operated sports organizations. This was fully funded by local taxes, donations, and fees.

During the entire time the internal war was being fought, the British tried to uphold the terms of the mandate and rejected any mention of majority rule that would allow the Muslim population, who were much control over Palestine.

CHAPTER SEVEN

The Ha'avara Agreement

The Jewish Agency and the Nazis negotiated a new agreement called the Ha'avara Agreement. Under this agreement, 50,000 German Jews were supposed to be transferred to Palestine.

The Germans confiscated their possessions, and the Ha'avara organization was to pay the Germans for goods worth 14 million pounds to be exported to Palestine. This was compensation for the immigrants.

Many Jews were ready to leave Nazi Germany but were afraid to. Those who left could not take any money and only allowed two suitcases. It was so bad that very few of them could afford the British entry tax.

The agreement was divisive.

Haim Arlosoroff, the Labour Zionist leader who negotiated the agreement, was assassinated in Tel Aviv in 1933.

The British used this assassination to create tension between the Zionist left and right.

Arlosoroff was the boyfriend of Magda Ritschel years before she married Joseph Goebbels. There was conjecture that the Nazis assassinated Arlosoroff to hide the connection between Arlosoroff and Magda. Unfortunately, there was never any evidence to back this assumption.

Jewish Immigration and the Ha'avara goods assisted in the growth of the economy. The tax paid by the Jews was used to build oil refineries and a seaport at Haifa and to fund their government in Transjordan. Industrialization began to overtake agriculture-dominated Palestine.

Between 1929 and 1938, more than 250,000 Jews immigrated to Palestine. About 174,000 Jews arrived between 1933 and 1936. After this, more than ever before, the British prevented immigration. Also, the British responded thus because of the Arab revolt that occurred between 1936 and 1939.

Most of the migrants who returned from Germany were professionals, doctors, professors, and lawyers.

Across Europe, many fascist regimes arose, and the persecution of the Jews increased. In many countries, Jews reverted to being non-citizens and were stripped of their basic human rights.

Anti-Semitic governments came to power in Poland, and Jews were placed on the embargo. By 1937, all Jews were excluded in many countries in Europe and Russia. Hungary, Romania, and the Nazis created states of Slovakia and Croatia while Germany annexed Austria and Czech zones.

Jerusalem Becomes an International City

Arab Revolt and the White Paper

The extensive riots between 1936 and 1936 in Palestine were largely due to the support of Nazi propaganda.

The riots were a separatist revolt that was targeted at ending British rule. Ben-Gurion, the leader of the Jewish Agency, responded to the Arab revolt with a policy of "Havlagah."

Havlagah is self-control and the refusal to respond to Arab attacks to prevent schism. The Etzel group, in opposition to this peaceful stance, broke off from Havlagah.

The Peel Commission in 1936-1937 was the British response. There was a public inquiry where approval was given to creating an exclusively Jewish territory near Galilee and the Western coast.

There was also meant to be a transfer of 250,000 Arabs so that every other area would be entirely Arab.

Chaim Weizmann and David Ben-Gurion were two recognized Jewish leaders. They persuaded the Zionist congress to approve the Peel recommendations to get the opportunity to negotiate a better deal.

The Palestinian-Arab leadership rejected the plan completely and began the revolt. The British then abandoned the plan.

When Weizmann testified at the Peel Commission, he said that 6 million Jews in Europe lived in a world where they were being stifled and threatened daily.

The US planned an international conference to talk about the many Jews who wanted to escape Europe to a haven.

The British refused to attend if Palestine was present. The Jews were not represented, and the Nazis insisted that the Jews be shipped to Madagascar to start a new life. The Madagascar Plan did not work, and so the Jews were trapped in Europe.

No country allowed the Jews to immigrate. The British decided to shut down immigration into Palestine.

There was a proposal to create an Independent Palestine that Arabs and Jews jointly ruled, and it was to be established in a decade. It was called the White Paper of 1939.

This plan allowed 75,000 Jews to migrate with Arab approval. This was to happen between 1940 and 1944. The Arabs and the Jews did not approve.

The British High Commission, on behalf of Palestine, then issued a decree stating that Jews were banned from purchasing land in 95% of Palestine.

Illegal immigration became the order of the day. With no external assistance and countries unwilling to help, few Jews fled Europe during the years when Hitler waged war against the Jews. This was the year 1939-1945.

Jews who the British escaping Europe caught were imprisoned in Mauritius.

World War II and the Holocaust

During the Second World War, the Jewish Agency developed a Jewish Army to help fight alongside the British. Winston Churchill was in support but could not get the government's support or that of its military.

The British insisted that there should be an equal number of Jewish and Arab recruits. Arabs refused to fight for Britain, and the Mufti of Jerusalem, the leader of Palestine, stood with Nazi Germany.

By 1940, Italy had declared war on the British Commonwealth and allied with Germany. Italian planes bombed Tel Aviv and Haifa.

The Jews created Palmach to defend the Jewish nation against the imminent attack coming from North Africa.

The British refused to arm the Jews.

When Rommel's forces were advancing via Egypt intending to occupy Palestine, the Jews were unarmed and seeming defenseless.

The Jews asked their youth to volunteer for the British Army, men and women. 30,000 Palestine Jews and 12000 Palestine Arabs were conscripted into the British Army.

By 1944, the decision to create a Jewish Brigade was agreed upon, and they were to fight in Italy.

More than a million Jews were a part of the allied armies worldwide, especially the United States and the Soviet Armies.

Within the Soviet Army, 200,000 Jews died in active service. About 200 activists committed themselves to resist the British. They broke away from Etzel and formed another group led by Avraham Stem. They were known as the Stem Gang.

When USSR released a Revisionist Zionist leader, Menachem, in 1943, he went straight to Palestine and took command of the Etzel organization. Another activist Yitzhak Shamir escaped from a camp in Eritrea where members of the Stem Gang were held without trial. He went to Palestine and took command of the Stem Gang.

The Second World War affected the Jews in the Middle East. Almost all of North Africa came under Nazi control, and the Jews in that terrain became slaves. A pro-Axis coup in Iraq led to the massacre of Jews.

The Nazis planned to annihilate all the Jews in Palestine. The Jewish Agency prepared for a fight to the death in case Rommel invaded Palestine.

In 1939-1945, the Nazi goal, supported by local forces, was to kill every last Jew in Europe. It was termed The Holocaust.

Six million Jews were annihilated when the war was over; 1.5 million of that number were children.

The Jewish communities and Polish communities disappeared.

The Jews in the US & Palestine lost track of their families in Europe. The Ashkenazi Jews were so affected that minority Jews, Sepharadi, and Mizrahi Jews gained significance.

The Jews who survived Europe were refugees. They told the Committee of Inquiry, consisting of British and Americans, that they preferred to return to Palestine. 95% chose Palestine.

Illegal Jewish Immigration and Insurgency

The war with the Middle East made the British weak. They became conscious of their dependence on Arab oil.

Britain was ruling over Kuwait, Bahrain, and the Emirates. Their companies controlled Iraqi.

After VE Day, the Labour Party won the general election, and even though they had longed backed the creation of a Jewish state, they instead went with the 1939 White Paper policies.

Buchenwald Survivors Arrive in Haifa to be Arrested By the British

The Jews came into Palestine illegally. A group called Bricha across Europe smuggled the survivors of the Holocaust into Palestine via the Mediterranean ports.

Jews in Arab countries came into Palestine overland.

When the war ended, the Jews in Palestine was almost 33% of the total population.

The Zionists began to use guerrilla tactics to fight against the British to gain their independence.

The Jewish Resistance Movement was formed when three Jewish factions agreed to work together. They are the Haganah, Etzel, and the Stem Gang. They allied to fight the British.

The King David bombings caused the alliance to divide.

The British launched Operation Agatha in 1946 and arrested over 2700 Jews plus the leadership of the Jewish Agency over alleged sabotage. Their headquarters were raided, and the prisoners were held without trial.

Another massive pogrom in Poland led to another large group of Holocaust survivors fleeing Europe in 1946.

Almost a month later, the bombing of the British Military HQ of the King David Hotel in Jerusalem by Iran resulted in the loss of 91 persons.

Curfew was declared in Tel Aviv, and about 120,000 people, 20% of the Jewish population, were taken in for questioning by the police.

The United States criticized how the British handled the incident and threatened to delay the British's loans to recover from the Second World War.

Almost 120,00 Jews left Poland between 1945 and 1948. The Zionists activities in Poland with support of the partial secret organization Berihah helped make their emigration possible. They helped plot an escape for the Jews from Hungary, Yugoslavia, Romania, and Czechoslovakia.

There were about 250,000 Holocaust Survivors rescued from Europe.

The British imprisoned the Jews who attempted to enter Palestine from the Atlit and the Cyprus concentration camps.

They were Holocaust Survivors, mainly large numbers of children and orphans.

The Jews began to allow Jews in 750 per month. This was done because the quota of 75,000 Jews according to the White Paper agreement of 1939 was never filled.

The Jews still lacked a state and documentation.

In 1947, the problem of the Palestine nation was finally the newly created United Nations.

CHAPTER EIGHT

United Nation's Plan

United Nations Partition Plan for Palestine

The General Assembly was to handle the question of Palestine by personal request of the United Kingdom.

A committee was created called the United Nations Special Committee on Palestine (UNSCOP).

The committee visited Palestine and met with Zionist and Jewish teams. The Arab Higher Committee was absent.

Ernest Bevin, the British Foreign Secretary, ordered the Exodus 1947, an illegal immigrant ship to return to Europe. In Hamburg, Germany, all the Holocaust migrants who had survived were forced to descend the ship.

Agudat Israel, the principal non-Zionist Orthodox Jewish party, recommended UNSCOP the possibility of setting up a Jewish State.

An agreement was also to be reached with Ben-Gurion that certain Jews, who were to attend religious seminary school and all women, be exempted from military service. The Sabbath would be a national weekend. There would be kosher food in all government institutions, and that Jews may be entitled to maintain a separate education scheme.

The majority of the UNSCOP proposed an independent Arab State, an independent Jewish State, and Jerusalem.

On November 29, 1948, an agreement was reached. The General Assembly had accepted most of the report by the UNSCOP with minor adjustments. The plan also stated that the British would allow a massive amount of Jewish migration by February of 1948.

They did not take any action from the resolution.

The British continued stopping the Jews who were attempting immigration into Palestine.

They were worried about the Anglo-Arab nations. The British refused to allow representatives of the United Nations entry to Palestine.

They adopted the resolution, the British Mandate was terminated, and then the British completed their withdrawal from Palestine in May 1948.

Britain continued to hold Jewish immigrants of the "fighting age" and their families in Cyprus until March 1949.

Civil War

This vote caused joy in the Jewish community and caused the Arabs to be discontented.

Civil war broke out.

From January 1948, the Arabs became battle-ready and consolidated their presence in Samaria and Galilee.

Egypt sent Abd al-Qadir al-Husayni with several hundred men of the Army of the Holy War. They recruited few thousand volunteers and organized a blockade of 100,000 Jewish residents in Jerusalem.

The Yishuy failed to supply the city using a convoy of 100 armored vehicles. Their vehicles were destroyed, and the blockade was held.

Many Haganah members attempting to bring supplies into the city were killed.

More than 100,000 Arabs from Haifa, Jaffa, and Jerusalem or the Jewish-dominated areas evacuated abroad or to Arab centers.

The US withdrew its support from the Partition Plan because of this incident.

The Arab League believed that the Palestinian Arabs, backed by the Arab Liberation Army, would silence the Jews and stop the plans being made for a partition.

On February 7, 1948, the British decided to back the invasion of the Arab part of Palestine by Transjordan.

The British commanded the Jordan Army.

CHAPTER NINE

The Independence of Israel

David Ben-Gurion restructured the Haganah and enlisted into the Army was compulsory.

Everyone was mandated to receive military training, including the men and women.

Golda Meir raised funds from Israeli sympathizers in the United States. Stalin backed the Zionist cause. With the money from these channels, they purchased arms in Eastern Europe to help fight for their freedom.

Ben-Gurion charged Yigael Yadin with the responsibility to plot the announcement of the intervention of the Arab states.

They planned to claim Jewish territory by conquering mixed zones.

Tiberias, Haifa, Safed, Beisan, Acre, and Jaffa fell.

This resulted in the 250,000 Palestinian Arabs taking flight. This was what caused all the states surrounding them to take action.

May 14, 1948, marked the day that the British forces left Haifa.

All the Jewish People's Council gathered at the Museum in Tel Aviv. They declared the creation of a Jewish state in Eretz Israel.

It was to be known as the State of Israel.

The Jews Fight the Six-Day War

Two world powers recognized the State almost immediately. They were the US President Harry S Truman and the Soviet leader, Joseph Stalin.

All the nations surrounding Israel refused to accept the UN Partition Plan. They stood with the Arabs across Palestine.

Transjordan, Egypt, Syria, Lebanon, & Iraq marched their armies into Israel and began the first Arab-Israeli war.

Although the Arab states had heavy military equipment, the Jewish State could not buy any heavy arms.

The British, on May 29, initiated a United Nations policy and declared an arms embargo on the region.

Czechoslovakia supplied the Jewish State with much-needed military hardware that could match the military hardware the Arabs were using, supplied by the British.

There was a truce of 4 weeks set in place by the UN.

Immediately after independence, the Haganah became the Israel Defense Forces (IDF). Finally, they had an army.

The security forces, Palmach, Etzel, and Lehi, were required to join the Army and cease any further secret operations.

Jews began arriving in Israel in large numbers. There were Holocaust survivors and war veterans. They immediately joined the IDF.

The Jewish State lost some territory and then gained up until July, when things turned around for them.

They fought and pushed the Arab armies back and took some part of the territory that belonged to the Arab State.

By November's end, an unconvincing ceasefire was arranged between Israel, Syria, and Lebanon.

King Abdullah announced the union of Transjordan with Arab Palestine west of Jordan. A lone Britain recognized the occupation.

Greenline

Israel signed a peace treaty with Egypt, Lebanon, Jordan, and Syria on February 24, March 23, April 3, and July 20.

Nothing was signed.

When the ceasefire came into effect, the border of Israel became known as the Green Line. The borders were unrecognized by the Arab states as international boundaries.

Israel controlled Jezreel Valley, Galilee, West Jerusalem, and the Negev.

Syria still controlled a strip of land along the Sea of Galilee. It was originally allocated to the Jewish State. Lebanon still occupied a small part of Rosh Hanikra. Egyptians still had the Gaza strip and had forces just outside Israeli territory. Jordan's Army remained in the West Bank, where the British stationed them.

After the ceasefire declaration, the British government release 2000 Jewish persons in their custody from Cyprus. They then recognized the State of Israel.

On May 11, 1949, Israel became a member of the United Nations.

They lost 6000 men and women in the fighting out of the 650,000 Jews who gathered. The 6000 Jews lost included 4000 soldiers in the IDF.

The United Nations records say that 726,000 Palestinians fled and were ousted by the Jews between 1947 and 1949.

The Palestinian refugees took cover in poor and crowded camps. Their host countries denied them citizenship.

The British then created another agency to provide aid for the refugees.

The 120-strong Knesset, who represents the Parliament of Israel, met first in Tel Aviv in 1949.

They held their first elections in January 1949.

The Socialist-Zionist won the most seats, and David Ben-Gurion was appointed Prime Minister.

A coalition was formed that did not include Mapam. The Mapam group were Stalinists and loyal to USSR. Maki, a non-Zionist party, won 4 seats.

This act signaled the fact that Israel would not be in the Soviet bloc.

The Knesset appointed Chaim Weizmann as the first President of Israel.

The official languages of the State of Israel were Hebrew and Arabic.

In the history of Israel, all governments are a result of alliances. No one party ever won a majority in the Knesset.

In the early years between 1948 and 1977, the Labour Party/Zionists and its predecessors led all governments.

In the first three years that Israel became a state, immigration doubled the Jewish population and influenced Israeli society.

More than 700,000 re-settled in Israel. About 300,000 came in from Asia and North Africa. The largest group of Jews that emigrated from the Arab nations back to Israel was about 100,000 people from Iraq.

Over 270,000 Jews came into the Israel State from Eastern Europe, particularly Romania and Poland, totaling 200,000.

The Jewish immigrants were mainly refugees. Amongst them, only 136,000 had international certifications.

They were a part of the 250,000 that were registered by the allies and displaced by the Second World War. They had lived in concentration camps in Germany, Austria, and Italy.

The Knesset passed a Law of Return in 1950 stating that all Jews and those with Jewish grandparents or spouses had a right to settle in Israel and get citizenship.

50,000 Yemenite Jews were brought into Israel covertly.

By 1951, Iraqi Jews numbering over 120,000 got permission to leave Iraq. 90% of them chose to move to Israel. More Jews fled Lebanon, Egypt, and Syria.

In the late sixties, almost 500,000 Jews left Algeria, Morocco, and Tunisia. Over the next twenty years, 850,000 Jews relocated to Israel, France, and America.

Land and property were left in Arab city centers, and this is still something that causes disagreements to date.

Today more than 9,000 Jews live in Arab states: 75% in Morocco and 15% in Tunisia.

Property and goods valued at $150 billion were left in the Arab states.

CHAPTER TEN

Life in Israel

A decade after Israel became recognized as a state, and their numbers grew from 800,000 to two million souls.

This was when food, clothes, and furniture were rationed in what was called the Austerity Period.

They lived in temporary camps.

More than 200,000 immigrants lived in tents or shacks.

Financial aid came from private donations from the United States, but there was great pressure on the new State's finances. This led Ben-Gurion to sign a reparation agreement with West Germany.

While the Knesset debated this issue, as many as 5000 demonstrators gathered and had to be restrained by riot police to keep them out of the building.

Israel received a billion marks and agreed to start diplomatic relations with Germany.

Ben-Gurion retired.

Education was made free and obligatory for all citizens until age 14 in 1949.

In 1952, an anti-Semitic public trial was staged in Moscow. A group of Jewish doctors was alleged to have attempted to poison Stalin. There was another kind of trial of this sort in Czechoslovakia.

Egypt closed the Suez Canal to Israeli ships and commerce in 1950. This was a violation of international law.

To solve diplomatic isolation, Israel established good relations with African states that had newly received their independence and France.

Moses Sharett became the prime minister of Israel at the head of a left-wing alliance in January 1955.

Sporadic clashes happened across Israel's borders between 1953 and 1956. There was constant Arab terrorism and breaches in the ceasefire agreement. This resulted in counter raids.

The Palestinian attacks were sponsored by the Egyptians and often came in through Gaza.

This became a cycle of violence, as Israel would respond to their attacks against Gaza.

Israel began using the Uzi submachine gun for Israel Defense forces in 1954. The Egyptian government also began recruiting prior Nazi rocket scientists for a missile program.

General Yigael Yadin, an archaeologist, purchased the Dead Sea scrolls for the State of Israel. They owned the entire first batch discovered. It is housed in the Shrine of the Book at the Israel Museum.

The Lavon Affair brought down Sharett's government. Israeli agents planted bombs at American sites in Egypt to destroy US-Egypt relations. The agents were arrested, and the Defense Minister was blamed. The Prime Minister retired, and Ben-Gurion became Prime Minister again.

Egypt purchased massive arms deal with Czechoslovakia in 1955, which would make them dangerous to other nations in the Middle East.

The following year, the Egyptian President announced that the Suez Canal, previously British-French-owned, now belonged to Egypt. They then blocked the Gulf of Aqaba to prevent Israel from accessing the Red Sea.

In response, Israel signed a covert agreement with the French to coordinate military operations against Egypt. Britain and France had already covertly begun preparing to carry out military operations against Egypt.

The French agreed to build a nuclear plant for the Israelis in 1968 to produce nuclear weapons.

Israel was to give the French and the British a reason to seize the Suez Canal. Israel would attack Egypt, and Britain and France would then intervene and ask them to withdraw.

When Israel attacked, and the French and Britain intervened, Israel refused to back down. The allies then began airstrikes on October 31, 1956. The goal was to neutralize the Egyptian Air force.

There was an uproar in the UN, and the US and USSR disapproving of Israel's actions, and her allies demanded a ceasefire, and one was accepted on November 7, 1956.

Egypt's request for emergency assistance of 6000 men from 10 nations marked the first peacekeeping mission ever.

The US assured Israel of access to the Suez Canal and demanded that Palestine stop the raids in Gaza. Israel then withdrew to the Negev. The Suez Canal remained close to Israeli shipping. This was the end of Western-European control in the Middle East.

In 1959, there were more clashes along Israel's boundary lines. This continued till the 60s.

The Arab League kept boycotting Israel economically and disagreements over water rights along with the Jordan.

The Soviet-backed the Arab states, while France backed Israel.

Eichmann Tried for War Crimes

Rudolph Kastner, a political figure, was accused of collaborating with the Nazis. He sued his accuser.

When he lost the trial, he was assassinated two years later. In 1958, the Supreme Court acquitted him.

In 1960, Mossad found a chief administrator of the Nazi Holocaust in Argentina. They kidnapped and brought him to Israel. He was put on trial, found guilty, and sentenced to death. Israel hung him in 1962. He is recorded as the only one ever found guilty in an Israeli court.

Israeli returnees at the trial told their stories. There was widespread publicity, and this trial was a defining moment in displaying the damage that the Holocaust had done to the public.

In 1962, Mossad began to assassinate German rocket scientists working on the missile program in Egypt. They had designed a missile that could carry chemical warheads.

Ben-Gurion disapproved of the assassinations, and the director of Mossad, Isser Harel, had to resign.

Six-Day War

In 1963, Israel fought the famous 6-day war.

It started with Yigael Yadin excavating Masada.

Jordan and Syria developed a united military command while Israel constructed a water carrier, an engineering project. Ben-Gurion's goal was to channel the water allocated to Israel from the Jordan to the South of the country. He wanted to achieve his dream of settling Israel's many migrants in the Negev desert.

The Arabs hatched a plan to divert the Jordan's waters, which led to fights between Israel and Syria.

The Indian Jews returned to Israel in 1964. Almost 2000 Jews from Cochin, India had migrated in 1954.

Until 1966, France supplied the arms that Israel needed. But after their withdrawal from Algeria, Charles de Gaulle declared that France would no more supply Israel with weapons. He also refused to refund the monies already deposited for warplanes.

The United States then declared that they would take over previous responsibilities of France and West

Germany and become responsible for making the Middle East stable in February 1966.

The necessary weaponry was over 200 tanks and one A-4 Skyhawk tactical aircraft given to Israel. They eased off security restrictions on Arabs and began to integrate them into Israeli life.

TV broadcasts began, and life began anew.

Two days later, Syria, Egypt, and Jordan rounded up their troops and closed the Straits of Tiran, blocking Israel from the seaports.

Nasser demanded UNEF leave Singi and threatened war.

Egyptian radio broadcasts led listeners to believe that the war's outcome would be the extermination of Israel.

On 26th May, the Egyptian leader said that their war was aimed at destroying Israel.

The nations surrounding Israel, Egypt, Syria, Jordan, and Iraq signed a defense pact, and they began to rally their troops. Algeria also allied with and sent troops to Egypt.

Between 1963 and 1967, Egyptian troops tested their chemical weapons on Yemenite civilians to support the rebels.

In response to the actions of the Arab nations, Israel called up its civilians to come and support them.

They stopped economic activities and started a National Unity Coalition. In a national radio broadcast, the Prime minister stammered and caused fear all over everyone in Israel.

Moshe Dayan, who had served Israel as Chief of Staff during the Sinai war, was appointed Defence minister.

Israeli air force launched tactical attacks destroying the Egyptian air force on the morning that Dayan was sworn in on 5th June 1967.

On that same day, they destroyed the air forces of Jordan and Syria. By 11th June, the Arab forces were in retreat, and everyone accepted the cease-fire called by the UN.

From this war, Israel gained new territories. Golan Heights, the Gaza Strip, the West Bank, and the Sinai Peninsula now belonged to Israel.

Israel occupied East Jerusalem, and those who lived there were given permanent resident status. They also had the choice of applying to be citizens of Israel.

The occupation was unrecognized internationally.

The Jordanian occupation was also unrecognized internationally. The only countries that acknowledged that occupation status was the UK, Iraq, and Pakistan.

In 1967, the Security Council created a formula for peace in the Middle East that required that Israel withdraw from territories they won in the 1967 war.

They reasoned that if Israel did this, all the troubles from the surrounding states would cease, and that would be respected for the sovereignty of all the states in the area.

Both sides accepted the resolution.

They both had different interpretations of the resolutions. This became the basis for negotiations hereafter.

After the 1967 war, the US supplied Israel with aircraft. The soviets broke diplomatic relations with Israel. Romania remained.

More pogroms in Poland encouraged the Jews resident there to return to Israel.

Jews now visited the Old City of Jerusalem to pray at the Wailing Wall.

Jordan had denied them access to this sacred site in violation of the 1949 peace treaty. The 4-meter wide alley was expanded into an enormous court.

For the first time in centuries, the worshippers could sit and make use of furniture.

The Jews in Hebron gained access to the Cave of the Patriarchs. They were allowed to pray at the entrance for the first time since the 1400s.

for the first time since the 14th century (previously, Jews were only allowed to pray at the entrance).[207] A third Jewish holy site, Rachel's Tomb, in Bethlehem, also became accessible. The Sinai oil fields made Israel self-sufficient in energy.

Moshe Levinger, along with a group of Religious Zionists, was honored to create the first Jewish settlement in Kiryat Arba.

They create a system for the education of every Jew until the age of 16. They enabled all children to be educated and provided the structures necessary. This system was in place until 2000.

In 1968, Land mines were placed on Israeli roads. Israeli forces then launched an attack on the Palestinian militia in Karameh, Jordan.

There were high fatalities on both sides. Yet Palestine claimed victory. In 1969, this time, the conflict was between Egypt and Israel over the Suez Canal.

Israel also responded to bombing from Egypt on Israeli forces along Suez Canal, and they made airstrikes in Egypt. They called it the War of Attrition.

When Levi Eschol died in office after have a heart attack, Golda Meir became the Prime Minister of Israel.

She carried the largest percentage of the vote ever won by an Israeli party. She won 56 of the 120 seats after the election in 1969.

Meir is credited with being the first female prime minister of Israel and the first to head a Middle Eastern state.

The Cherbough Project

In 1969, Israeli naval commandos entered Cherbourg Harbour in France at night. They came in and took the boats that Israel had paid for, and France refused to supply.

By 1970, they shot down soviet fighters who were supporting Egypt in the War of Attrition.

The US tried to calm the situation, and they both agreed on a cease-fire.

King Hussein of Jordan drove the Palestinian Liberation Organization (PLO) out of his country in September 1970.

By 1970, Syria came to Jordan with tanks to help the PLO.

The US requested that Israel march their troops to the border as a threat to Syria. Syria withdrew.

The PLO began to operate in Lebanon. The area where the PLO operated was called "Fatahland," which led to the civil war in 1975-1990.

Hafez al-Assad also took power in Syria for this reason. In Egypt, Anwar Sadat took over from Nasser, who died from a heart attack immediately afterward.

There was more hatred for the Jews in the soviet, and more Jews came home in droves. In the usual manner, they were only allowed two suitcases and their properties confiscated.

They were not provided with exit visas; some were arrested and sent to the Gulag.

They began to call the survivors of the Gulag "Prisoners of Zion."

During the Munich Olympics in 1972, two of their teammates were killed, and nine were taken as hostages by Palestinian terrorists.

Germany bungled the rescue, and the rest of them were killed along with five of the eight hijackers.

West Germany released the remaining three Palestinian hijackers without any charges laid against them. This they did in exchange for the hostages of a hijacked Lufthansa Flight.

Israel responded by an air raid on the PLO headquarters in Lebanon. There was a bounty placed on the head of the organizers of the Massacre.

The new president in Egypt, Anwar Sadat, ousted the Soviet advisers from Egypt. Israel grew complacent about the threat that Egypt and Syria posed to her.

Israel did not want to be accused of making trouble in the Middle East and did not rally their forces even when they received warnings of an imminent attack.

CHAPTER ELEVEN

Yom Kipper War

The Yom Kipper War happened in October. It began on 6th October 1973. It happened on one of the holiest days on the Jewish calendar, and it was a day separated for fasting.

Syria and Egyptian forces launched surprise attacks against the Israeli Defense Forces.

For the first few days, it was uncertain if Israel would be able to resist the invaders.

Both Soviets and the Americans dispersed weapons to their allies.

Israel repelled the Syrians using their tanks on the Golan. Although Egypt captured a small territory in Sinai, Israel crossed Suez Canal and trapped Egypt's army in Sinai.

Two thousand people died in Israel and made Israel aware of the dangers to their nation.

After this war, Egypt and Israel were more willing to negotiate.

The Israeli and Egyptian governments, on 18th January 1974, agreed on a Disengagement of Forces agreement. Henry Kissinger deliberated on the issue with the two parties. The same kind of agreement was made with Syria on 31st May 1974.

A Saudi-led oil embargo was placed on the nations that traded with Israel. This resulted in many countries breaking relations with Israel.

Israel could not participate in the Asian Games and any of its sporting events.

In 1974, Palestinians took hostage 102 children from a school in the Ma'a lot. They killed 22 of them.

By November of 1974, the PLO was granted observer status, and Yasser Arafat talked with the General Assembly.

The Agranat Commission was appointed to assess the charge for Israel's lack of readiness for war.

The Chief of Staff and head of military intelligence took the fall. The public was so angry that Golda Meir resigned as prime minister of Israel.

Yitzhak Rabin, who was chief of Staff during the six-day war, became prime minister.

In November 1975, under the guidance of Kurt Waldheim, the Austrian Secretary-General of the United States, they adopted a resolution that affirmed Zionism as a form of racism. In December 1991, they rescinded their decree.

A massive strike by Israeli-Arabs stopped the government's plan to confiscate land in Galilee in March 1976.

In July, Palestine struck again and hijacked 260 people in an Air France plane. The hijackers were a mixture of Palestinians and Germans. They flew the hostages to Uganda, where Idi Amin ruled at the time.

While in Germany, the Germans sifted the Jews from the non-Jews and released the latter.

The French crew refused to leave. The Germans then proceeded to threaten the 100 Jewish passengers along with the French crew.

Rabin ordered a daring rescue operation. The kidnapped Jews were freed. It was a violation of the sovereignty of a United Nations member state. The UN Secretary-General Waldheim said as much to Uganda.

Waldheim was a suspected war criminal and a former Nazi. He made a habit of offending Jewish sensibilities.

There was a civil war in Lebanon in 1976. In line with this information, Israel allowed South Lebanese to cross the border to work in Israel.

Abu Daoud, a man who planned the Munich Massacre, was arrested in France in January 1977. They released him shortly after.

In November 1977, history was made when Anwar Sadat, the President in Egypt, broke over 30 years of hostility and visited Jerusalem at the invitation of the current prime minister in Israel, Menachem Begin.

His visit included a speech before the Israeli government and a turning around in the history of years of conflict.

Egypt's president changed the thinking of the countries in the Middle East and made peace between Israel and its Arab nations possible.

He recognized the right to exist as a nation and opened the door to future negotiations between Egypt and Israel.

After his visit, 350 Yom Kippur veterans organized a "Peace Now" drive to inspire the government to make peace with the Arabs.

Palestine hit again. This time they came to Israel in boats and hijacked a bus carrying families on a fun trip. They killed 38 people and 13 children. They opposed the peace process between Egypt and Israel.

Three days later, Israel began Operation Litani. Israel had earlier withdrawn its troops at the behest of the United Nations.

Camp David Accords

President Carter invited the leaders of Israel and Egypt to Camp David to meet with him.

On 11th September, President Sadat and Prime Minister Begin agreed on a framework for peace between Israel and Egypt and to complete peace in the Middle East.

Broad principles were set to guide their negotiations. Guidelines for all territories were also decided upon.

They signed the treaty on 26th March 1979, and the United States president signed as a witness.

With the new treaty, Israel handed the Sinai Peninsula back to Egypt in April 1982. They gave Egypt every land that was due to them.

The Arab League responded by suspending Egypt from its organization. They moved their HQ from Cairo to Tunis.

Islamic fundamentalist members of the Egyptian army assassinated the Egyptian prime minister in 1981.

With the agreements signed, Egypt and Israel became the recipients of US military and financial aid.

In 1979, 40,000 Iranian Jews escaped into Israel to escape the Islamic revolution.

On 30th June, the Israeli air force destroyed Osirak, a nuclear reactor. France was building it for Iraq.

High tech industries sprung up in Israel in the 1980s.

Following the treaty with Egypt, PLO began to attack Israel from South Lebanon.

The Lebanese government claimed PLO was independent.

In June 1982, Shlomo Argov, the Israeli ambassador to Britain, escaped an attempted assassination. Israel took this opportunity to drive the PLO out of the southern half of Lebanon. They called it the 1982 Lebanon War.

The Israeli army occupied Beirut. The Shia and Christian population in Lebanon welcome Israelis as PLO had victimized them for a long.

Over time, the Lebanese grew resentful of Israeli occupation. They then radicalized the Shia Muslims.

Constant casualties of Israeli soldiers and civilians in Lebanon led to growing resistance to the war in Israel.

The PLO withdrew its forces from Lebanon and moved to Tunisia in August 1982.

The president of Lebanon, Bashir Gemayel, agreed to a peace treaty with Israel. He was assassinated before any agreement could be signed.

A day later, in Phalangist, Elie Hobeika led Phalangist Christian forces into a refugee camp and slaughtered all.

Four hundred thousand began a demonstration almost immediately. They gathered in Tel Aviv. They were unanimous in voicing their displeasure against the war.

After a public inquiry, it was discovered that Defense minister Sharon was responsible for the massacres.

Lebanon and Israel signed an agreement in 1983. Israel was to withdraw from Lebanon in stages. Israel continued operating against the PLO. They eventually left in 1985 and left a garrison of soldiers in South Lebanon to support the South Lebanon army until 2000.

By October, Israel responded to a Palestinian terrorist attack in Cyprus by blowing to blazes the PLO HQ in Tunis.

In August 1987, Israel had to cancel a Lavi project. It was a trial in making an autonomous Israeli aircraft. The developmental costs were huge.

They also faced opposition from the US, who wanted to retain military dominance and their influence in Israel.

The Israel State sent a satellite into space. They used a Shavit rocker and became one of the eight countries with the capacity to launch satellites. They have since launched two more.

In 1990, the Soviet Union finally permitted Jews to emigrate to Israel. Before this time, the Jews who left faced immense persecution, those that succeeded left as refugees. The massive emigration changed the atmosphere in Israel and brought many educated Jews who translated their powerful Russian culture into Israel.

Iraq invaded Kuwait and acted as a catalyst for the Gulf War.

The fight was between Iraq and a large allied force with the United States at the head. Iraq fired 39 scud missiles at Israel.

The United States asked Israel not to respond to provoke the other Arab nations from joining the fight.

Gas masks were provided for the Israel and Palestine population by the US government.

15,000 Beta Israeli were covertly airlifted into Israel over a day and a half.

When the coalition won the victory in the Gulf War, new possibilities for the Middle East were seen. Mikhail Gorbachev and George HW Bush, the Premier of the

Soviet Union and the US president, assembled a historic meeting in Madrid, Spain.

Israeli, Lebanon, Jordanian, Syrian, and Palestinian leaders were present. At first, the prime minister disagreed but was persuaded by loan guarantees to help him settle the new wave of immigrants from the Soviet Union.

When he participated in this conference, the right-wing coalition in Israel collapsed.

NEW WORDS

Beta Israel are Ethiopian Jews.

CHAPTER TWELVE

Striving for Peace

In the elections held in Israel in 1922, the Labour party won a significant number of seats.

What was significant was that the parties that supported a peace treaty had a majority vote in the Knesset.

In the latter part of the year, the electoral system changed to allow the direct election of the prime minister. This system was abandoned in 2006 because it was flawed.

In 1993, Israel carried out a 7-day military operation in Lebanon to attack Hezbollah.

Israel and the PLO signed an Oslo Accord on the South Lawn of the White House.

The principles had the aim of the transfer of authority from Israel to an interim Palestinian Authority. It was the beginning of the final treaty to establish a Palestinian state and both Israel and Palestine would be recognized.

They fixed May 1999 as the date for a permanent pact for the West Bank and Gaza Strip to take effect.

But in February of 1994, Baruch Goldstein, a follower of the Kach party in Israel, killed 29 Palestinians and wounded 125 of them. This gory scene took place at the Cave of the Patriarchs in Hebron.

Israel had previously ruled that the Kach group were racist, so they were not allowed to participate in elections. They finally made the group illegal.

The agreement was signed in Gaza in May 1994. Israel and the PLO signed what is known as the Jericho agreement. They also signed the Agreement on Preparatory Transfer of Powers and Responsibility in August.

Israel and Jordan signed an agreement called the Washington Declaration. This ended their state of war from 1948. It was signed on 25th July 1994.

On 26th October, another treaty was signed by Israel and Jordan and witnessed by President Bill Clinton.

PLO Chairman Yasser Arafat and the Prime Minister of Israel Yitzhak Rabin signed the Israeli-Palestine Interim Agreement on the Gaza Strip and the West Bank on 28th September 1995. Bill Clinton witnessed this agreement on behalf of the United States. It was also witnessed by Egypt, Norway, Russia, and the European Union.

This treaty incorporated and superseded any previous agreement. This was the conclusion of the first stage of the negotiations between the PLO and Israel.

According to the agreement, the PLO leadership could be relocated to occupied territories, and autonomy was granted to Palestine and further talks.

Palestine gave their word that they would no longer use terror, and they changed the Palestinian National Covenant. Their old covenant called for the ejection of all the Jews who immigrated to Israel and the destruction of every Jew.

Hamas opposed the agreement. Other Palestinian factions also opposed the agreement and sent suicide bomber attacks to Israel.

The prime minister made a barrier around Gaza to prevent the attacks.

The separation between Israel and Palestine caused a labor shortage in Israel, especially in the construction industry.

Israel imported laborers from the Philippines, Thailand, Romania, and China. They stayed in Israel even without visas.

Africans in a large number began illegally migrating to Israel for work.

On 4th November 1995, Prime Minister Yitzhak Rabin was assassinated by a far-right-wing Zionist. They were challengers of the Oslo Accords.

In February 1996, Shimon Peres, who succeeded the Prime Minister after his death, called for early elections.

NEW WORDS

The Oslo Accord is a Declaration of Principles.

Palestine's Subterfuge

In 1996, in May, the first elections that could elect a prime minister were carried out in Israel, resulting in a narrow victory.

Binyamin Netanyahu, a Likud leader, became the next prime minister.

After a series of suicide bombings in Israel, they were convinced that security was a priority for Israel.

Despite his disagreements with the Oslo Accords, he implemented them. The peace process still slowed down. He set out to limit US aid to Israel.

In September 1996, a riot broke out to protest the construction of an exit in the Western Wall tunnel. Eighty people were killed over the next couple of weeks.

In January, Netanyahu signed the Hebron Protocol with the Palestinian Authority. This resulted in the posting of Israeli forces away from Hebron and the handover to civilian authority and Palestinian Authority.

In the election of July 1999, Ehud Barak became prime minister.

In September of the same year, the Supreme court ruled that using torture to interrogate Palestinians who were imprisoned was illegal.

Pope John Paul II visited Israel in March 2000.

In May 2000, Israel withdrew their forces from Lebanon. Thousands of the South Lebanon Army, along with their families, left with the Israelis.

By 16th June 2000, the United Nations acknowledged that Israel had withdrawn its forces.

Lebanon alleges that Israel still occupies a part of the Lebanese territory known as "Sheba's Farms."

Hezbollah used the excuse of Sheba's Farms to keep fighting with Israel.

Lebanese government broke international laws by not taking authority over the area and leaving it for Hezbollah to rule over.

Talks at Camp David to reach a final agreement on the Israel-Palestine conflict held in the fall of 2000.

Ehud Barak agreed to meet the demands of the Palestinian teams for territory and for making allowances when it came to politics, including the Arab parts of Jerusalem.

Arafat abandoned the talks and did not make a counterproposal.

Israel became a member of Western Europe and Others Group in the United States after withdrawing its troops from Lebanon.

Before this time, Israel belonged to no groups because Arab nations did not allow them to join the Asia group. So it was limited from having any key roles at the UN. From December 2013, Israel has been a stable member.

Opposition leader Ariel Sharon visited the Temple Mount on 28 September 2000. The next day, Palestinians launched an Intifada. In October 2000, the Palestinians destroyed Joseph's Tomb.

The Peace Process was in confusion.

Ehud Barak called a special election for Prime Minister. He thought he would win so that he could continue Palestinian negotiations, but opposition leader Ariel Sharon became prime minister.

This was the last election where they used this system of directly electing the Premier.

Palestinian terror attacks increased. Hezbollah attacked Israel occasionally from Lebanon.

This caused Israel to lose confidence in ever having Peace with Palestine.

Israelis, in a large number, could not wait to extricate themselves from Palestine.

There was a wave of suicide bomb attacks, and the grand finale was when many were massacred during the Passover Feast. It was called the Passover Massacre.

Operation Defensive Shield was launched in March 2002. Sharon started constructing a barrier around the West Bank.

Palestine kept shelling an Israeli Town called Sderot and other communities. They also experienced mortar bomb attacks from Gaza.

Jews from Latin America immigrated to Israel in this season. There was an economic crisis in the countries they were coming from.

In 2004, Black Hebrews were granted a long-lasting residency in Israel. They had been migrating to Israel for 25 years from the United States. They were not recognized under Israel's Law of Return until 2004.

In 2004, Sharon's government created a system that helped in the construction of desalinization plants, and these helped give citizens confidence as it concerned drought. Their desalinization plants are the largest anywhere in the world.

Operation Rainbow was started in May 2004 in Gaze to create a safer environment for Israel's soldiers along the Philadelphi Route.

They launched Operation Days of Penitence to destroy the sites from which Palestine sent rockets to hurt Israeli towns.

Jewish settlers in Gaza were forcefully evacuated from Gaza and their homes wiped out.

The disengagement from the Gaza Strip ended on 12 September 2005. Ten days later, they finished disengaging their military from the West Bank.

Is Peace in the Middle East Possible?

Sharon left the Likud and joined a party that supported the peace process.

In Palestine, Hamas won the elections. They claim that this is the first and only sincerely free and fair elections.

Hamas' leaders rejected all the agreements that were signed with Israel. They went back on all the agreements from the right of Israel to exist and any other promise.

They claimed that the Holocaust was a Jewish conspiracy. They clung to terror as a tool they would employ at will.

The Hamas victory and the withdrawal of troops from Gaza left everyone unclear on their position.

Israel vowed that it was no longer an occupying power, yet they still controlled air and sea access to Gaza. It did not exercise dominion over the land.

Egypt maintained that it was still being occupied and closed the borders. It was free too.

Ariel Sharon had a stroke and was weakened. Ehud Olmert became the prime minister.

He was elected again in 2006.

Mahmoud Ahmadinejad became elected President in Iran in 2005. The Iranian policy towards Israel progressively became aggressive.

Analysts in Israel are convinced that the President of Iran undermines the peace process by funding Hezbollah in South Lebanon and Hamas in Gaza.

They believe that he is developing nuclear weapons to use against Israel.

Iranian support for Hezbollah and its nuclear arms program violates UN Security Council resolutions. Iran also claims that the Holocaust is a conspiracy.

Israel withdrew from Lebanon, and Hezbollah maintained intermittent attacks. Israel refused to respond.

The withdrawal from Gaza also led to the shelling of the towns situated outside Gaza. Israel responded minimally.

The right-wing of Israel criticized the lack of Israeli response. This undermined the Israeli government.

Israel carried out a military operation in the Palestinian Authority prison of Jericho to capture a Palestinian Arab prisoner called Ahmad Sa'adat and others. These men were responsible for assassinating an Israeli politician in 2001.

The Hamas government had communicated their intentions to release the prisoners.

When a Hamas force crossed the Gaza border in March 2006 and attacked a tank, capturing Israeli soldier Gilad Shalit, it sparked fights in Gaza.

NAHAL BRIGADE SOLDIERS RETURNING AFTER THE 2006 LEBANON WAR

Hezbollah once again attacked from Lebanon. They shelled Israeli towns and attacked border control. They took two dead and some badly wounded Israeli soldiers.

This caused the start of the Second Lebanon War. It lasted through August 2006.

Israeli forces went into Southern Lebanon, and the air force attacked targets all over the country.

Israel did not make much progress on the ground until they launched Operation Changing Direction. This lasted three days with doubtful results.

A ceasefire was effected shortly. Then Israeli captured Wadi Saluki. As the war ended, Hezbollah retrieved its forces from Lebanon. The Israeli forces remained until they handed over to the Armed Forces in Lebanon.

A casino owner who is a billionaire, Sheldon Adelson, set up a newspaper to break the influence of the only other paper and supported Netanyahu.

In June 2007, Hamas claimed the Gaza Strip during the battle in Gaza. They replaced government officials with their own.

Egypt and Israel imposed a partial blockade.

The Air force declared a nuclear reactor in Syria on 6 September 2007.

On the 288th February 2008, Israel responded to the constant firing of Qasam rockets by Hamas militants and launched a military campaign.

Hezbollah asked to exchange Israeli soldiers Ehud Goldwasser and Eldad Regev for Lebanese terrorist Samir Kuntar in July 2006. They also asked for four Hezbollah prisoners and the bodies of 199 Palestinian Arab and Lebanon fighters. Hezbollah swapped the bodies and gave them different people.

Operation Cast Lead was carried out in the Gaza Strip in December 2008. They were responding to Hamas militants who kept up with the rocket attacks. This led to a decrease in rocket attacks.

Billionaire Yitshak Tshuva announced the discovery of huge natural gas reserves off the coast of Israel.

Direct negotiations between Palestine and Israel brooked no success again in September 2010.

Israel began to operate an advanced mobile air defense system, the Iron Dome, in the Southern region of Israel and along the border with the Gaza Strip.

This was deployed as a defensive countermeasure to the rocket hazard against Israel's civilian population.

CHAPTER THIRTEEN

What Has Ever Changed?

Protest in Tel Aviv on 6 August 2011

The largest social protest since Israel became a state happened on 6 August 2011. There were hundreds of thousands of Israelis from all demography and all socio-economic backgrounds and religious leanings. They were protesting the rising cost of living, especially housing.

They also protected the deterioration of public services in the country.

The demonstrations reached their heights on 3 September 2011, where about 400,000 people demonstrated all over Israel.

Israel and Hamas reached an agreement in October 2011. The kidnapped soldier, Gilad Shalit, was released.

Israel got him back and had to give Palestine 1027 Palestine and Arab-Israeli prisoners.

The Secretary-general of the Popular Resistance Committees, Zuhair al-Qasi, a senior PRC member and two militants from Palestine, were assassinated in March 2012. It was a targeted murder carried out by Israeli forces in Gaza.

Armed factions in Gaza Strip and other militia groups fired a substantial amount of rockets towards southern Israel in retribution. This provoked five days of endless skirmishes along the Gaza border.

Israel transported the bodies of 91 suicide bombers and other militia as a humanitarian gesture to Palestine. The Chairman of the PA, Mahmoud Abbas, received them. It was a gesture to help spark off another round of peace talks or new negotiations with Palestine.

Israel responded to hundreds of rocket attacks on southern Israeli cities; Israel started Operation Gaza on

14 November 2012. They targeted Ahmed Jabari, the chief of Hamas military wing, and sent airstrikes against 20 underground sites that were used to house long-range missile launchers.

These weapons could strike Tel Aviv.

The construction of the barrier on the Israeli-Egyptian was completed.

Benjamin Netanyahu was elected Prime Minister.

In 2013, Israel agreed to release more than 100 Palestinian prisoners as a goodwill gesture to begin peace talks. They had been in jail since the 1993 Oslo Accords, along with other militia who killed Israeli civilians.

In April 2014, peace talks were suspended after Hamas agreed to form a united government with Fatah.

The rockets Hamas used to attack the cities around Gaza Strip escalated again. Israel started an operation targeted at destroying the cross-border tunnels that Hamas used in fighting.

New elections in 2015 resulted in Netanyahu being the Prime Minister.

Palestine released a wave of lone-wolf attacks on Israel between 2015 and 2016. It was mainly stabbings.

Trump Announces Recognition of Jerusalem As The Capital Of Israel

On 6 December 2017, the President of the United States, Donald J Trump, officially recognized Jerusalem as the capital of Israel.

He then recognized Golan Heights as part of Israel on 25 March 2019.

Palestinians in Gaza initiated "the Great March of Return," which were weekly protests on the Gaza-Israel border.

In April 2020, in the middle of the coronavirus pandemic, and after three

In April 2020, amid the coronavirus pandemic and after three sequential elections under the space of 12 months, a unity government was established by Benjamin Netanyahu and Benjamin Gantz.

It is a unity government with features of a rotating prime minister-ship. Netanyahu would serve first and then hand over to Gantz.

Towards the end of 2020, Israel regularized relations with four Arab nations, namely: the United Arab Emirates and Bahrain, in September. It was called the Abraham Accords.

Then they normalized relations with Sudan in October and Morocco in December.

CONCLUSION

Who knew that Israel and Palestine had a history that long and that painful?

Hopefully, there is clarity on what drives these two different nationalities and who seem to be at war longer than they have been at Peace.

Will the peace accords hold?

No one can say categorically. But we are keeping our fingers crossed and hoping for more years of Peace for these people groups. They deserve it.

ABOUT THE AUTHOR

Michael James is a renowned historian and an advocate for peace in the Middle East. He has closely followed the dispute in the Middle East. As a result, he has a vast knowledge of all the happenings that have led to present-day events. Authoring this 'The Israeli and Palestinian Conflict' is his way of sharing this knowledge with the reader.